RIGHT TO COUNSEL

Gideon v. Wainwright (1963)

By MARK E. DUDLEY

TWENTY-FIRST CENTURY
BOOKS
A Division of
Henry Holt and Company

New York

To Mark, Jeff, and Leon.

Twenty-First Century Books
A Division of Henry Holt and Company, Inc.
115 West 18th Street
New York, NY 10011

Henry Holt® and colophon are trademarks of
Henry Holt and Company, Inc.
Publishers since 1866

Library of Congress Cataloging-in-Publication Data
Dudley, Mark E.
Gideon v. Wainwright (1963) : right to counsel / Mark E. Dudley. — 1st ed.
p. cm. — (Supreme Court decisions)
Includes bibliographical references and index.
Summary: Examines the people, events, and legal issues involved in the Supreme Court case that established the right of people to be represented by a lawyer even if they cannot afford to pay.
1. Gideon, Clarence Earl—Trials, litigation, etc.—Juvenile literature. 2. Wainwright, Louis L.—Trials, litigation, etc.—Juvenile literature. 3. Right to counsel—United States—Juvenile literature. 4. United States—Supreme Court—Juvenile literature. [1. Gideon, Clarence Earl—Trials, litigation, etc. 2. Wainwright, Louis L.—Trials, litigation, etc. 3. Right to counsel.]
I. Title. II. Series: Supreme Court decisions (New York, N.Y.)
KF228.G53D83 1995   345.73'056— dc20   94-40885
[347.30556]   CIP AC

Photo Credits
Photo on page 44 courtesy of Bruce R. Jacob.
Photos on pages 68 and 72 © Flip Schulke, Black Star.
All other photos provided by AP / Wide World Photos.

Design
Tina Tarr-Emmons

Typesetting and Layout
Custom Communications

ISBN 0-8050-3914-7
First Edition 1995

Printed in the United States of America
All first editions are printed on acid-free paper ∞.

10 9 8 7 6 5 4 3 2 1

Contents

The Bill of Rights

Amendment I

Congress shall make no law respecting an establishment of religion, or prohibiting the free exercise thereof; or abridging the freedom of speech, or of the press; or the right of the people peaceably to assemble, and to petition the Government for a redress of grievances.

Amendment II

A well regulated Militia, being necessary to the security of a free State, the right of the people to keep and bear Arms, shall not be infringed.

Amendment III

No Soldier shall, in time of peace be quartered in any house, without the consent of the Owner, nor in time of war, but in a manner to be prescribed by law.

Amendment IV

The right of the people to be secure in their persons, houses, papers, and effects, against unreasonable searches and seizures, shall not be violated, and no Warrants shall issue, but upon probable cause, supported by Oath or affirmation, and particularly describing the place to be searched, and the persons or things to be seized.

Amendment V

No person shall be held to answer for a capital, or otherwise infamous crime, unless on a presentment or indictment of a Grand Jury, except in cases arising in the land or naval forces, or in the Militia, when in actual service in time of War or public danger; nor shall any person be subject for the same offence to be twice put in jeopardy of life or limb, nor shall be compelled in any criminal case to be a witness against himself, nor be deprived of life, liberty, or property, without due process of law; nor shall private property be taken for public use, without just compensation.

Amendment VI

In all criminal prosecutions, the accused shall enjoy the right to a speedy and public trial, by an impartial jury of the State and district wherein the crime shall have been committed, which district shall have been previously ascertained by law, and to be informed of the nature and cause of the accusation; to be confronted with the witnesses against him; to have compulsory process for obtaining witnesses in his favor, and to have the assistance of counsel for his defence.

Amendment VII

In Suits at common law, where the value in controversy shall exceed twenty dollars, the right of trial by jury shall be preserved, and no fact tried by jury, shall be otherwise reexamined in any Court of the United States, than according to the rules of the common law.

Amendment VIII

Excessive bail shall not be required, nor excessive fines imposed, nor cruel and unusual punishments inflicted.

Amendment IX

The enumeration in the Constitution, of certain rights, shall not be construed to deny or disparage others retained by the people.

Amendment X

The powers not delegated to the United States by the Constitution, nor prohibited by it to the States, are reserved to the States respectively, or to the people.

Amendment XIV (ratified July 28, 1868)

Section 1. All persons born or naturalized in the United States, and subject to the jurisdiction thereof, are citizens of the United States and of the State wherein they reside. No State shall make or enforce any law which shall abridge the privileges or immunities of citizens of the United States; nor shall any State deprive any person of life, liberty, or property, without due process of law; nor deny to any person within its jurisdiction the equal protection of the laws.

Section 2. Representatives shall be apportioned among the several States according to their respective numbers, counting the whole number of persons in each State, excluding Indians not taxed. But when the right to vote at any election for the choice of electors for President and Vice President of the United States, Representatives in Congress, the Executive and Judicial officers of a State, or the members of the Legislature thereof, is denied to any of the male inhabitants of such State, being twenty-one years of age, and citizens of the United States, or in any way abridged, except for participation in rebellion, or other crime, the basis of representation therein shall be reduced in the proportion which the number of such male citizens shall bear to the whole number of male citizens twenty-one years of age in such State.

Section 3. No person shall be a Senator or Representative in Congress, or elector of President and Vice President, or hold any office, civil or military, under the United States, or under any State, who, having previously taken an oath, as a member of Congress, or as an officer of the United States, or as a member of any State legislature, or as an executive or judicial officer of any State, to support the Constitution of the United States, shall have engaged in insurrection or rebellion against the same, or given aid or comfort to the enemies thereof. But Congress may by a vote of two-thirds of each House, remove such disability.

Section 4. The validity of the public debt of the United States, authorized by law, including debts incurred for payments of pensions and bounties for services in suppressing insurrection or rebellion, shall not be questioned. But neither the United States nor any State shall assume or pay any debt or obligation incurred in aid of insurrection or rebellion against the United States, or any claim for the loss or emancipation of any slave; but all such debts, obligations and claims shall be held illegal and void.

Section 5. The Congress shall have power to enforce, by appropriate legislation, the provisions of this article.

An Attorney for Everyone

Clarence Earl Gideon, a poor man from Missouri with little education, was convicted of burglary in Florida, despite his pleas that he had not committed the crime. He insisted he had not had a fair trial because he had been unable to afford an attorney to represent him and the county court had refused to provide him with one. He appealed his case to the U.S. Supreme Court, where he was represented by the well-known attorney Abe Fortas.

On March 18, 1963, the U.S. Supreme Court agreed with Gideon that everyone was entitled to counsel. Those too poor to hire their own attorney, the Court ruled, must be provided one by the state. That ruling changed the lives of many poor people accused of crimes and guaranteed the right to counsel to all.

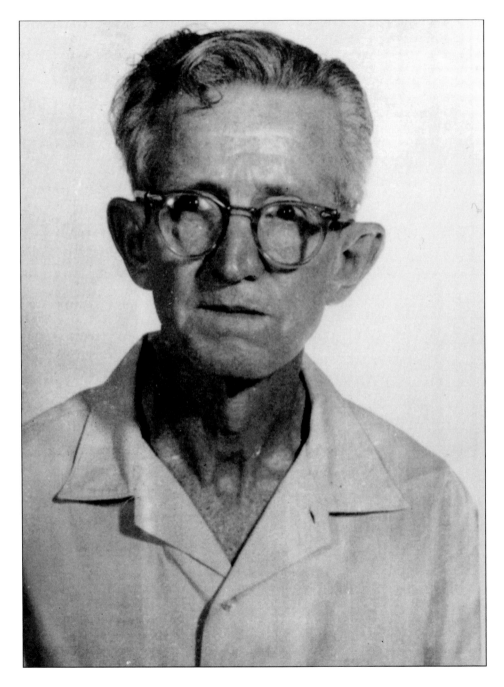

Clarence Earl Gideon in 1963

CHAPTER ONE

Bay Harbor Poolroom

I believe that each era finds a[n] im-
provement in law, each year brings
something new for the benefit of
mankind.[1]

—**Clarence Earl Gideon**

Ira Strickland Jr. was not thinking of his place in history as he locked the door of his pool hall at the end of a long day. The Bay Harbor Poolroom on the outskirts of Panama City, Florida, was not frequented by movers and shakers. In 1961, Bay Harbor consisted of the poolroom, a bar, a seedy hotel, and a few other run-down buildings. Strickland couldn't have been too surprised to discover a deputy sheriff waiting for him when he returned to work the following morning. Sometime after midnight, someone had smashed a window and robbed the place. The culprit had broken into the vending machines for the change and had stolen beer, wine, and soda.

Officer Henry Berryhill Jr. discovered the break-in on a routine patrol. He asked a man hanging around the front of the building if he knew anything about the robbery. The man, Henry Cook, told the policeman that he had seen Clarence Gideon, a local man, leaving the building. Berryhill called the deputy sheriff, Duell Pitts Jr., to the scene. Pitts listened as Cook repeated his story. The deputy found Gideon later that morning in a downtown Panama City bar. Despite his pleas of innocence, Gideon was arrested for the burglary.

Clarence Gideon was not a model citizen. He was a poor white man whose familiarity with legal proceedings resulted from his numerous scrapes with the law. He realized he had little chance of proving his innocence by himself. Juries and judges rarely believed the word of a poor man with a criminal record. Yet he could not afford to hire a lawyer to assist him.

Gideon had been guilty of many things in his life. When caught and punished, he accepted that as his fate. But he hadn't broken into the poolroom, and he wasn't willing to suffer the consequences of a crime he hadn't committed. He was determined to pursue his right to a fair trial.

Gideon was not an educated man. He was not a crusader. Yet he strongly believed that he deserved justice. It was that belief that led him to challenge the way trials were conducted in this country—a challenge that would end up in the United States Supreme Court.

Clarence Earl Gideon was a stooped and broken-looking man. Life had been hard on him, and it showed in his white hair and trembling hands and voice. He was born in 1910 in Hannibal, Missouri. His father died when he was three, and his mother remarried two years later. His mother and stepfather were factory workers. Though poor, they provided a decent home for Clarence. Gideon rebelled against their strict discipline, however, and left home at age fourteen.

For the next 33 years, Gideon roamed the country. He worked at an assortment of odd jobs, which were interrupted by numerous stays in prison, usually for burglary. He was married four times. In 1957, Gideon moved his family to Panama City, seeking to escape from his criminal record. He supported his wife and five children by working as a mechanic, but he soon found himself in jail again.

Gideon was fond of gambling and usually did quite well at it. He made the mistake of winning too much from a game run by a local police commissioner. Arrested on trumped-up charges, Gideon was denied his request for a lawyer to represent him. The judge eventually found him not guilty, and he was released. While he was in jail, his wife struggled to feed their children. The state welfare officials finally placed the children in foster homes.

Out of jail, Gideon worked with a local church to reclaim his children. Soon after winning custody of his children, he became too ill to care for them. Tuberculosis kept him in the hospital for months. When he returned home, he found that his wife had left him and had given the children up to the authorities. Gideon arranged to send money to the welfare department to help support the children. He worked at odd jobs, but he was too sick and had too long a criminal record to make much money. Once again, he turned to gambling to make his living.

Shortly before the poolroom burglary, Gideon was arrested twice for crimes he hadn't committed. The FBI believed he was guilty of a break-in at the local armory because he had been convicted of a similar crime 25 years before. When the Bay Harbor Bar was robbed, police suspected Gideon, who lived in the run-down hotel across the street. Finding no evidence in either case, the police threw him into jail for vagrancy. A month after his release, on June 3, 1961, Gideon was arrested for breaking into the Bay Harbor Poolroom.

Gideon's trial was held in the Circuit Court of Bay County, Florida, on August 4. Judge Robert L. McCrary Jr. began the proceedings by asking

Gideon if he was ready for trial. The defendant replied that he was not. When asked why not, Gideon said, "I request this court to appoint counsel to represent me in this trial."[2]

The judge explained that under Florida law, he couldn't appoint a lawyer to defend Gideon unless he was accused of murder or some other capital offense. A capital offense is one that carries a possible sentence of death. "The United States Supreme Court says I am entitled to be represented by counsel,"[3] Gideon responded.

The Supreme Court had ruled in a 1932 case that the states had to provide lawyers for poor people charged with serious crimes like murder. In a 1938 case the Court ruled that poor defendants, regardless of the seriousness of the charges against them, were entitled to lawyers in federal trials. But Gideon was being tried for a minor offense in a state court. Judge McCrary took note of the request but refused it and continued the trial.

McCrary asked the six jurors if they would "give him the same fair trial, and consideration, since he is not represented by counsel, that you would if he were represented."[4] They replied that they would. Next he asked Gideon if he accepted those jurors, or if he would like any of them replaced. Gideon was unaware that he could question the jurors to see if any might be prejudiced against him. He accepted the panel of jurors.

The prosecutor, Assistant State Attorney William E. Harris, presented the case against Gideon. On the stand, Henry Cook testified he had seen Gideon, whom he knew, inside the poolroom the morning of the burglary. Cook claimed that Gideon came outside carrying a bottle of wine. Then, according to Cook, Gideon called a taxi from the corner phone booth and left.

Gideon did his best to cross-examine the witness. He inquired why Cook was outside the poolroom at 5:30 A.M. Cook said he was returning from a dance in another city. Gideon wanted to know if Cook had ever been convicted of a felony. Cook said no. The cross-examination did little to help Gideon's cause.

Strickland testified next. He told how he had locked up the poolroom at midnight on June 2 and returned the next morning to find the deputy and a broken window. Strickland told the court that the vending machines had been robbed of their coins. Beer, wine, and soda were also missing. Gideon fared no better cross-examining Strickland.

Gideon presented eight witnesses for his defense. Officers Berryhill and Pitts told their stories. Their testimony established only that the officers had relied on Cook's word as to Gideon's guilt. Gideon neglected to emphasize that fact to the jury.

Preston Bray, the cabdriver who had given a ride to Gideon, was next. In response to Gideon's question—the only one he asked of Bray—the cabdriver testified that Gideon wasn't drunk the night of the robbery. Actually, it would have been helpful to Gideon's case to prove the opposite—drunkenness was a proper defense for such a crime in Florida. When the prosecutor cross-examined the driver, Bray mentioned that Gideon had been working at the poolroom. In fact, Gideon sometimes ran a poker game for the manager there. Gideon could have pointed out that, being an employee of sorts, he might have had an excuse for being in the poolroom. He even had keys, so there was no reason for him to break into the building. Unfamiliar with legal tactics, Gideon didn't pursue this line of reasoning.

Next, Gideon questioned a neighbor, Irene Rhodes. She testified that she had seen Gideon coming from the alley by the pool hall that morning. A defense attorney certainly would not have solicited such testimony. She did say that it wasn't uncommon to see Gideon using the phone at the corner.

Several other witnesses added little. Gideon's landlady took the stand last. She confirmed that Gideon often went out at night to use the phone. She also said that she had never seen him drunk. Gideon made a final plea of his innocence to the jury and rested his case.

Judge McCrary's instructions to the jury were brief. He didn't explain the elements of the crime, as a defense attorney might have requested. The jury wasted little time in finding Gideon guilty. After reviewing Gideon's record, McCrary sentenced him to the maximum sentence, five years, at the state prison in Raiford. Gideon had no chance to argue for a reduced sentence.

He could, however, appeal his conviction. Gideon didn't dispute any procedural errors unique to his case. If he had been able to recognize such flaws, he would have done so at the trial. Instead, he claimed that the trial itself was unconstitutional, because he wasn't provided with an attorney. "I knew the Constitution guaranteed me a fair trial," Gideon said, "but I didn't see how a man could get one without a lawyer to defend him."[5]

By state law, constitutional claims were pursued by petitioning the Florida Supreme Court to issue a writ of habeas corpus. This is a legal order requiring officials to deliver a prisoner before a court to investigate whether he or she is being held illegally. The Latin name of the writ means "you should have the body."

Gideon sent his request to the state supreme court soon after his conviction. On October 30, 1961, the court passed judgment. The justices refused to review the circuit court's verdict. They gave no reason. Their decision simply read, "The above-named petitioner has filed a petition for writ of habeas corpus in the above cause, and upon consideration thereof, it is ordered that said petition be and the same is hereby denied."[6] Gideon had only one avenue of appeal left—the United States Supreme Court.

The warden and prison staff were sympathetic to prisoners pursuing a legal claim. Convicts appealing their cases were usually well behaved. As an assistant warden put it, "Our feeling is, 'Boys, if you can get out of here legal, we're with you.'"[7] But it was not easy to prepare a legal case while in prison. There were no resources, no law library or attorneys to consult, not even a typewriter. Prisoners were restricted to sending two letters a week. Gideon had picked up a slight knowledge of legal proceedings from his many scrapes with the law, though, and did the best he could. He even helped other prisoners, many of them illiterate, with their appeals.

Gideon's first attempt to contact the Supreme Court was a failure. So many petitions are received by the Court that it requires strict adherence to the proper forms. Forty copies of the petition must be sent, and all supporting documents must be typed. Petitioners have to pay a fee—$100 in 1961. Because not everyone can afford such requirements, the Court exempts poor petitioners from paying the fee and producing the copies. Such applicants have to provide an affidavit stating that they can't afford to fulfill the usual requirements. Gideon had neglected to send such a document.

The court clerk who returned Gideon's letter enclosed a copy of the Supreme Court rules. Gideon's next try was successful. The court clerk opening the convict's letter found the notarized affidavit, a copy of his appeal to the Florida Supreme Court and the court's reply, and his main petition. This was titled "Petition for a Writ of Certiorari Directed to the Supreme Court of Florida." A writ of certiorari is an order that the certified records of the last court to hear the case be forwarded to the court of appeals.

Gideon's document was handwritten and full of incorrect grammar and spelling. Its intent was clear, though. Gideon described his alleged crime and sentence. Then he claimed that his rights under the Fourteenth Amendment of the U.S. Constitution had been violated. The Fourteenth Amendment guarantees all citizens that the government will not "deprive any person of life, liberty, or property, without due process of law. . . ."[8] Gideon believed that due process included the right to be represented by a lawyer. As he explained in his petition, "When at the time of the petitioner's trial, he ask[ed] the lower court for the aid of counsel, the court refused this aid. Petitioner told the court that this [U.S. Supreme] Court made [a] decision to the effect that all citizens tried for a felony crime should have aid of counsel. The lower court ignored this plea."[9]

Actually, the Court's past decisions had established very narrow and vague conditions indicating when counsel was required. The current justices were uncomfortable with that policy. They had been waiting for a chance to clarify the law. They were under no obligation to hear Gideon's case. The vast majority of appeals to the Supreme Court are turned down. Normally, the justices agree with the lower court's ruling or believe the complaint too trivial for the Supreme Court to decide. Only rarely will they consider reversing a decision that the Supreme Court has already made.

An accused person's right to counsel was an issue whose time had come. On June 4, 1962, the justices granted a hearing to Gideon. His appeal would be heard under the name *Gideon v. Cochran*. H. G. Cochran was the director of the Florida Division of Corrections—Gideon's jailer. The name of the case was later changed to *Gideon v. Wainwright* when Louis L. Wainwright replaced Cochran as director of the prison system. The case was scheduled for the following autumn. Clarence Earl Gideon would have his day in court.

CHAPTER TWO

Constitutional Rights

*Of all the rights that an accused per-
son has, the right to be represented by
counsel is by far the most pervasive,
for it affects his ability to assert any
other rights he may have.[1]*

—Judge Walter V. Schaefer

Few citizens are immune to the arms of our modern
penal code; federal, state, and local laws control every aspect of our daily
lives. Many statutes are remnants of another age's values. So-called blue
laws, outlawing activities such as running a business on Sunday, are still on
the books in some places. These laws are usually universally ignored.
However, law enforcement officials may enforce them if they choose.

Other regulations are highly complex. Some business laws require
extensive research to ensure compliance. Activities permitted in some
states are banned in others. For example, some western states allow people
to drink alcoholic beverages while driving. A person inadvertently crossing
a state line while doing so could very well end up in jail.

Almost anyone may face court proceedings. At the time of Gideon's

Leaders of the new American republic sign the Constitution of the United States.

arrest, more than ten million cases were heard and more than one million Americans were convicted every year. Between 30 and 60 percent of these people were too poor to afford a lawyer. People attempting to defend themselves competently need to be familiar with hundreds of volumes of law books. Obviously this is beyond the capability of the average citizen. Poor people are even worse off. Frequently with little education, or even illiterate, they can hardly be expected to mount an effective defense. Yet the right to counsel is a recent addition to the annals of law.

When the United States split off from Great Britain in the eighteenth century, the new government took with it the legacy of English common law. Under these traditions, people accused of serious crimes weren't allowed any representation at all. They could not testify before the court or call witnesses for their defense. Even the charges against them were kept secret until their trial.

The framers of the U.S. Constitution, who had so recently been on the wrong side of English law, tried to rectify this injustice. They set up a system of three branches of government. The legislative branch was given the task of making the laws. The executive branch was charged with enforcing those laws. And the judicial branch interpreted the laws—that is, the courts were to apply the written law to specific cases. By dividing responsibilities in this way, the founding fathers hoped to prevent any one faction from abusing its power.

Article 3 of the Constitution establishes a Supreme Court and lower courts to interpret the law. The article lists the types of cases to be considered by these courts and requires these cases to be tried by a jury. It also states that decisions of the lower courts may be appealed to the Supreme Court.

Further legal rights are spelled out in amendments to the Constitution.

The first ten amendments, collectively known as the Bill of Rights, were passed by the state legislatures soon after the Constitution was ratified.

The Sixth Amendment, in particular, spells out proper criminal procedure. People accused of crimes have the right to know what charges are made against them. Trials must be conducted in public. No secret testimony is allowed—witnesses must face the accused. People speaking for the accused may be forced to appear in court. Perhaps most important is the assurance that citizens have the right to be assisted by counsel. The amendment does not say, however, that attorneys will be provided for those who cannot afford to hire their own.

One of the thorniest problems to be worked out by the founders was the question of states' rights versus federal power. About half the founders believed that a strong central government was necessary to maintain control and defend the citizenry. An equally strong contingent, still smarting from the authoritarian rule of King George III, preferred to give most of the power to the individual states.

The final form of the Constitution struck a balance between these two factions. Article Six established the Constitution as the supreme law of the land. The states' courts had the duty to interpret and apply the Constitution to their own citizens. The states were allowed to make their own laws and establish their own courts as long as these laws and courts were not in conflict with federal law. Federal courts could hear only cases involving the nation as a whole, quarrels between states or citizens of different states, and cases "arising under this Constitution."[2]

In the 1800s, this clause was interpreted to allow the Court to declare state laws and lower court decisions unconstitutional. But, until the 1920s, the Court went along with the theory that only the Constitution, not the Bill of Rights, applied to the states.

States' rights backers believed the Bill of Rights amendments should apply only to the federal government. James Madison, the principal author of the Bill of Rights, believed the document should also apply to the states. He introduced an amendment guaranteeing that, "No state shall infringe the right of trial by jury in criminal cases, nor the rights of conscience, nor the freedom of speech, or of the press."[3] The proposal was rejected by the Senate. In the 1833 case *Barron v. Baltimore*, the Supreme Court specifically stated that the Bill of Rights didn't apply to the states.

The states' power to regulate their own citizens became less popular as antislavery sentiment spread. Abolitionists wanted the federal government to ban slavery in all the states. In the wake of the Civil War, the Fourteenth Amendment was passed. Ratified in 1868, it was meant to guarantee that the newly freed black man have the same rights as the white man. The amendment stated that:

> No State shall make or enforce any law which shall abridge the privileges or immunities of citizens of the United States; nor shall any State deprive any person of life, liberty, or property, without due process of law; nor deny to any person within its jurisdiction the equal protection of the laws.[4]

Civil liberties proponents believed that the Fourteenth Amendment was meant to include the Bill of Rights in the privileges it guaranteed to citizens. They argued that the Fourteenth Amendment did what Madison had proposed to do in his failed amendment—it required that the states grant citizens the rights specified in the Bill of Rights.

Others, however, did not agree with that interpretation of the Fourteenth Amendment. They argued that it applied only to the Constitution and not to the Bill of Rights. Until the 1920s, the Supreme Court agreed with this second view of the Fourteenth Amendment. The Court did not overrule state laws and practices that denied the provisions of the Bill of Rights to their citizens.

The tide began to turn in the mid-1920s. The Court decided that free speech—guaranteed by the First Amendment—was so basic a right that states could not restrict it without violating the Fourteenth Amendment. As time went on, the Court required other provisions of the Bill of Rights to apply to the states. Still, they resisted specifically stating that the privileges granted by the Bill of Rights were automatically protected by the Fourteenth Amendment.

In particular, the Court adopted a hands-off position in regard to the five amendments covering the process of criminal law. The Sixth Amendment, providing for a fair trial and "the assistance of counsel,"[5] was no exception. However, in 1932 the Court decided that in some circumstances, states must provide counsel. It took the extreme injustice of the infamous Scottsboro case to spur the justices to act.

CHAPTER THREE

Previous Right-to-Counsel Cases

That which is simple, orderly, and necessary to the lawyer, to the untrained layman may appear intricate, complex and mysterious.[1]

—Justice Hugo L. Black

Scottsboro, Alabama, in 1931, was a hotbed of racial prejudice. As a freight train approached the small town on March 25, a mob of angry whites waited at the station. They had received word that a group of nine young black men riding the train had fought with some young white men a few hours earlier. Who started the fight and what really happened was unclear. The blacks had thrown the whites from the train. When the black men arrived in town, they discovered that they were accused of raping two white women who had been riding with the white men. The crowd's mood was ugly. The sheriff, fearing a lynching, took the accused men to the next town to await trial. Within a few days, fifteen-year-old Ozie Powell and his fellow defendants were tried and sentenced to death.

The presiding judge made sure the defendants couldn't find an attorney easily. He appointed all the members of the local bar to assist in the prosecution. Sympathetic observers appealed the conviction and pursued the case to the U.S. Supreme Court. The case was officially known as *Powell v. Alabama.*

The Court found that the Scottsboro boys, as they were called, had been denied a fair trial. The defendants had been so grievously wronged that the Court ruled they had been denied the due process of law guaranteed them by the Fourteenth Amendment.

Justice George Sutherland, writing for the Court, noted that an untrained defendant "lacks both the skill and knowledge adequately to prepare his defense, even though he have a perfect one. He requires the guiding hand of counsel at every step in the proceedings against him. Without it, though he be not guilty, he faces the danger of conviction because he does not know how to establish his innocence. If that be true of men of intelligence, how much more true is it of the ignorant and illiterate. . . ."[2]

Reviewing the specifics of this case, the justices decided that the defendants had been denied the time and opportunity to find attorneys to represent them. The Court went even further to protect the accused men's rights. The Court's opinion stated, "In a capital case, where the defendant is unable to employ counsel, and is incapable adequately of making his own defense because of ignorance, feeblemindedness, illiteracy, or the like, it is the duty of the court, whether requested or not, to assign counsel for him as a necessary requisite of due process of law."[3] Not only were defendants to be allowed a chance to obtain a lawyer, but the lower courts were obliged

Defendants in the Scottsboro case are shown on November 22, 1933, leaving Morgan County Jail in Decatur, Alabama, on their way to their retrial. The Supreme Court overturned their conviction in the first trial.

to provide one for them. This was the first time the Supreme Court had ruled that, in some cases, the Constitution required states to provide counsel.

Sutherland took pains to limit the decision. The Court had never reversed a state court decision in a criminal case due to an unfair trial before. It was the particular nature of the Scottsboro case—the obvious prejudice of the trial judge and the townspeople, and the finality of the death sentences—that necessitated the Supreme Court's action.

The next important decision involving the right to counsel took place in 1938. This was a counterfeiting case known as *Johnson v. Zerbst*. Because this was a federal case, the Sixth Amendment clearly applied. The Court held that defendants in all federal trials were entitled to court-appointed counsel, regardless of the severity of the crime, if they couldn't provide an attorney themselves. Previously, lawyers were provided only if the offense was a serious one.

The year 1942 brought the next landmark right-to-counsel case. Smith Betts was charged with robbery in a case similar to the one that Clarence Gideon would face 21 years later. Too poor to afford counsel, Betts asked the Maryland judge to appoint a lawyer. The judge denied Betts's request. Maryland law provided for counsel for poor people only in murder and rape cases. Like Gideon, Betts did the best he could to defend himself, but he was convicted and decided to appeal the decision through the state courts.

The U.S. Supreme Court finally heard the case as *Betts v. Brady*. The Court rejected Betts's argument that the Sixth Amendment applied to the states. The only question to be considered, the Court ruled, was whether Betts had been deprived of a fundamental right necessary to a fair trial under the Fourteenth Amendment. The justices first considered the intent

Justice Hugo L. Black

of the authors of the Bill of Rights. Historical evidence indicated that the founders were not concerned with providing counsel for the poor. They had been mainly interested in rejecting the English common law that prohibited all accused felons from having an attorney.

The Court then considered the attitude of the individual states toward providing counsel for the poor. There was no consensus. Some states mandated or allowed appointed counsel in all cases. Some provided lawyers only in capital cases. The justices decided that the right to counsel was not fundamental. Justice Owen Roberts, writing for the Court, said that the Fourteenth Amendment did not include "an inexorable command that no trial for any offense, or in any court, can be fairly conducted and justice accorded a defendant who is not represented by counsel."[4]

The opinion also noted the social consequences of applying the Sixth Amendment to the states. Even traffic cases and civil suits might require appointment of lawyers. The cost would be enormous.

The Court concluded by recognizing that lack of counsel might sometimes result in an unfair trial. That would have to be decided on a case-by-case basis. They determined that Betts, a reasonably intelligent man with some knowledge of criminal proceedings, was capable of conducting his own defense. The charges against him were straightforward. There were no extenuating circumstances. His conviction would stand.

Three of the justices disagreed with the majority opinion. Justice Hugo Black believed that the authors of the Fourteenth Amendment had intended that the Sixth Amendment rights apply to the states. Denying counsel to the poor seemed to him "to defeat the promise of our democratic society to provide equal justice under the law."[5]

Black was not alone. There was widespread criticism of the *Betts v. Brady* ruling in the press. Both the public and the bar called for reversing the opinion. Especially in light of the ongoing abuse of human rights in Nazi Germany and the Soviet Union, the decision seemed an affront to democratic principles in the United States. A letter to the *New York Times* shortly after the *Betts* ruling was strongly critical of the decision. "The decision in *Betts v. Brady* comes at a singularly inopportune time," the letter read. "Throughout the world men are fighting to be free from the fear of political trials and concentration camps. From this struggle men are hoping that a bill of rights will emerge which will guarantee to all men certain fundamental rights . . . [including] the right of the accused person to have the assistance of counsel for his defense."[6]

The Court was not immune to the criticism. Justice Felix Frankfurter defended the decision by predicting that, if *Betts* was overturned, there would be a widespread release of prisoners convicted without benefit of counsel.

The Court considered other right-to-counsel cases on the basis of "special circumstances" affecting the fairness of the trial. These circumstances were listed in the opinion written by Justice Stanley F. Reed in the 1948 case *Uveges v. Pennsylvania*. Reed wrote, "Where the gravity of the crime and other factors—such as the age and education of the defendant, the conduct of the court or prosecuting officials, and the complicated nature of the offense charged, and the possible defenses thereto—render criminal proceedings without counsel so apt to result in injustice as to be fundamentally unfair . . . the accused must have legal assistance."[7]

The Court routinely overturned convictions in capital cases where the accused didn't have an attorney.

The *Uveges* ruling did little to guide lower court judges in deciding when to require attorneys. Judges had no clear idea what comprised special circumstances. Even the Supreme Court's distinctions between what were and were not special circumstances were vague and contradictory. In 1948, the Court issued two rulings on the same day—one reversed a conviction in a right-to-counsel case, and the other upheld a conviction of a defendant who had had no attorney.

In *Gryger v. Burke*, the judge had misinterpreted a state law that he

32 Justice Felix Frankfurter

thought called for a mandatory life sentence. Despite the judge's mistake, the Court ruled against Gryger. Apparently, the Court believed that the outcome would have been the same even if Gryger had had an attorney.

In *Townsend v. Burke*, the trial judge had mistakenly believed Townsend had had two prior convictions and gave him a harsh sentence as a result. The justices decided that a lawyer might have corrected the judge's mistaken view. They ruled in favor of Townsend.

The distinctions between the two cases were not convincingly logical. It was clear that the *Betts* decision was inadequate. Lower court judges had no way of knowing which special circumstances would require a lawyer and which would not. Without a specific guideline to use, they had only conflicting Court decisions on which to base their rulings.

It is the legislature's job to make laws and to amend or revoke them. A judge can declare a law void only when that law conflicts with a prior statute or the Constitution. Justices rarely decide a case on the intrinsic rightness or wrongness of a law. They rely on precedent—previous rulings—to apply a law to a specific case. Courts are always reluctant to overturn prior rulings.

Once a ruling is made, all lower courts are required to abide by it. The Court will overturn a ruling only if there are powerful, overriding reasons. These two great principles—the universality and the constancy of law—allow the orderly functioning of society. Citizens must know what to expect in order to avoid breaking the rules.

The principle of following precedent is known as stare decisis. The term comes from the Latin phrase *stare decisis et non quieta movere*. This means "to adhere to precedents, and not to unsettle things which are established."[8]

So great is the Supreme Court's commitment to this doctrine that it has overturned prior Court rulings only about 100 times in its 200-year history. Over the years, the public may change its opinion about what rules are acceptable in society. When this happens, the legislatures and the courts must respond. But it is extremely difficult for the legislature to reverse a Supreme Court ruling. At such times, the responsibility for what could be far-reaching consequences falls upon the shoulders of the nine justices.

In the years before *Gideon*, the Court reluctantly approached the decision to overturn *Betts*. Gradually, the special circumstances calling for appointment of counsel were widened to include more and more conditions. For example, some states have laws allowing tougher sentences for people who have a prior criminal record. The Court decided that these laws were so complex that convicts accused of a second crime needed an attorney to help them interpret the laws.

In a 1947 case, *Adamson v. California*, four of the nine justices voted that the Fourteenth Amendment extended the protection of the Bill of Rights to citizens in state courts. If Adamson had won the case, the Court would have required states to abide by the Sixth Amendment. The majority of the justices, however, declined to infringe on states' rights to that degree.

In 1961, in *McNeal v. Culver*, the Court reversed an assault conviction because of the complexity of Florida law. In a concurring opinion on the case, Justices William J. Brennan Jr. and William O. Douglas called for the overruling of *Betts*. They based the reversal of McNeal's conviction not only on the due process clause of the Fourteenth Amendment, but also on the amendment's equal protection clause. They believed that a poor defendant deserved as competent a defense as a rich one.

This approach was also seen in a 1956 case, *Griffin v. Illinois*. In *Griffin*, the Court struck down an Illinois law requiring appellants to pay for the trial transcripts of their trials that they needed to provide to the appeals court. Poor people couldn't afford to pay the transcript copying fees, and thus couldn't appeal.

One other case was pivotal in laying the groundwork for overturning *Betts*. As recently as 1949, the Court had been unwilling to require the states to abide by the ban on illegal search and seizure guaranteed by the Fourth Amendment in federal cases. In the 1961 case *Mapp v. Ohio*, the Court overturned its prior ruling and declared that illegally obtained evidence could not be used in state trials. The justices' willingness to reject precedent in the face of dire warnings of massive prisoner releases and loss of states' rights showed new courage.

The Fourth Amendment was now a universal requirement. Soon the Court would have to consider the Sixth Amendment's guarantee of the right to counsel. Since 1950, the Supreme Court had overturned every case before it where a defendant had been convicted without legal representation. The time was ripe to tackle *Betts* head-on.

Abe Fortas, the lawyer who represented Clarence Gideon before the U.S. Supreme Court

CHAPTER FOUR

Gideon's Defense

It seemed to me the responsibility was not just to try to win the case but to get as many justices as possible to go along. . . .[1]

—**Abe Fortas**

Gideon had no trouble having an attorney appointed for his Supreme Court hearing. The Court always appoints counsel for poor people who request it. It is a mark of great distinction to be asked to represent an appellant before the Court. Few turn it down, though there is no payment for the service. Generally, the justices pick an attorney of national reputation.

Abe Fortas was well-known in Washington, D.C. He was a successful corporate lawyer who also had experience in criminal law. For a time he had served as undersecretary of the interior. Fortas already had represented several clients before the Supreme Court. He was acquainted with Chief Justice Earl Warren and Justices Douglas, Brennan, and Black. When called upon to represent Gideon, Fortas readily accepted.

Fortas was appointed Gideon's counsel on June 25. His office began working on the case soon afterward. Fortas's first dilemma was trying to decide on what grounds to defend Gideon. Fortas recognized that the Court was prepared to overturn *Betts*, given a good enough argument. That was clearly the trend of Supreme Court right-to-counsel rulings since *Betts*. But his first duty was to Gideon, not to a constitutional question.

If he could prove that there were special circumstances requiring appointment of counsel in Gideon's particular case, Gideon would probably win. But it would be a hollow victory for everyone else. *Betts* would not be overturned on such narrow grounds. The Court's decision wouldn't apply to other prisoners. Fortas fervently believed that the right to counsel was a basic right. He needed to overturn *Betts* to correct the injustice that had doubtless sent hundreds of innocent people to jail.

Fortas asked that the Florida officials send him a transcript of Gideon's trial. There was little in the transcript to suggest that there was any impropriety in the proceedings. Gideon had presented a reasonably competent defense for a layman. The judge had obviously tried to protect his rights. The charges against Gideon were straightforward. No serious errors had occurred in the trial.

Fortas decided to ask Gideon for some background information. In particular, he wanted to know if Gideon was black. Members of minorities often suffered prejudicial judgments in the South. Gideon sent Fortas a long letter, detailing his life, his prior record, and his grievances with the criminal justice system.

Fortas found scant evidence of any special circumstances. Clarence Gideon himself appeared to agree. "It makes no difference how old I am or what color I am or what church I belong to if any. The question is I did not get a fair trial. The question is very simple. I requested the court to appoint me [an] attorney and the court refused, . . ."[2] he had written the Court the previous spring.

Fortas decided the way was clear to prepare a defense on constitutional grounds. One problem facing the lawyer was how to get the evidence before the Court. The Supreme Court requires that a printed copy of the lower court records and the decision being appealed be supplied to them. Technically, Gideon hadn't appealed the decision the judge rendered at the end of his trial. He was protesting the legality of the trial itself. As a result, the only official record before the Court was his habeas corpus petition and the Florida Supreme Court order rejecting his appeal.

Fortas wanted to present Gideon's trial transcript to the justices. This was the strongest evidence that *Betts* should be overturned. John Hart Ely, an intern with Fortas's law firm, put it best:

> At first blush, the transcript in *State v. Gideon*
> seems to present the very model of the myth of
> *Betts*; a case in which defense counsel is not
> needed. For the defendant exhibited remark-
> able skill in cross-examination, and the judge
> went to great lengths to inform him of his
> rights. . . . Yet even here close examination of
> the law and of the facts reveals that defendant
> was repeatedly hurt by lack of counsel. If such
> prejudice occurred in this trial, it would seem
> that there is *no* trial in which counsel is unnec-
> essary.[3]

Fortas sent the Court clerk a list of the records he wanted to be submitted for the hearing. As required, a copy was forwarded to Bruce Jacob at the Florida attorney general's office for suggested additions or deletions. Soon Jacob sent a reply.

Jacob argued that the trial transcript shouldn't be included in the record. "Matters which took place at the trial which were not alleged in the petition for habeas corpus are not involved in the instant case and therefore have no place in the printed record,"[4] he wrote. Fortas was allowed to respond to the protest. He pointed out that the Court could review whatever evidence it wished. Surely what took place at the trial was relevant.

Two weeks after the Supreme Court began its term in October 1962, the justices handed down their order. The trial transcript would be allowed. Fortas now had 30 days to submit his brief to the Court. A brief is the written document presented to the court containing the facts and arguments of a case.

Fortas began his brief by stating that the special circumstances rule of *Betts* had done little to assure fair trials in the vast majority of cases. Without lawyers present during trials, errors continued to be made. Fortas argued that keeping *Betts* would not advance the cause of states' rights. Indeed, he said, it yielded the opposite result. Without a clear rule guiding the state courts, prisoners would continue to appeal their convictions, and federal judges would continue to reverse state judges' decisions.

Fortas followed with five main sections supporting Gideon's case. First, he argued that the Fourteenth Amendment required that counsel be provided to poor people as a fundamental right. The complexity of modern law demanded the assistance of counsel. Federal law required this, and state law was no less complicated, he argued. Even criminal lawyers charged with crimes rarely undertook their own defense.

Judges might try to safeguard the defendant's rights, but that was not their main task, Fortas wrote. They could hardly be expected to do a thorough job of it. And there was always the chance of a conflict of interest.

Although the states had appointed counsel in capital cases since the Scottsboro case, there was no real logic to this. Noncapital cases could well be more complex than capital ones. The Fourteenth Amendment, Fortas noted, protected liberty and property, as well as life. Fortas also brought up the equal protection argument, citing the Court's decision in *Griffin v. Illinois*. The Court had ruled that defendants too poor to afford copying fees were as entitled to trial transcripts as wealthier people. By the same logic, they should have the same opportunities for representation by counsel, Fortas argued.

The brief's second section dealt with the issue of states' rights. In the 20 years since *Betts*, many states had changed their policies. Currently, only 13 states didn't require counsel for poor people charged with felonies. Eight of those states routinely provided counsel anyway. Florida did so in some cases. Trial judges in some Florida cities always appointed attorneys for the poor. And 24 states mandated counsel even for misdemeanor charges.

Since the majority of states saw fit to provide poor people with counsel, states' rights wasn't much of an issue, Fortas argued. Forcing the consensus of the majority of states on the few holdouts was a small imposition. In *Mapp v. Ohio*, Fortas noted, the Court had forced fully half the states to abide by the search-and-seizure rules of the Fourth Amendment.

Fortas mentioned the great number of appeals made by prisoners who had been tried without counsel. Federal judges continually had to overturn state court decisions due to violations of *Betts*'s special circumstances rule. Surely, this constant intrusion on states' sovereignty was harmful to states' rights, Fortas contended. Even if the court ordered the states to provide counsel, the states would still be free to devise a system of their choosing to comply with that order.

The third section dealt with the problems caused by the vagueness of the *Betts* ruling. Studies had shown that the states rarely found any special circumstances requiring counsel. Fortas cited the case of a retarded Pennsylvania man. The man was judged to be capable of defending himself in court even though his mental age was that of a child of nine. The Supreme Court itself was inconsistent in determining what circumstances indicated the need for counsel. Surely, argued Fortas, it was too much to ask of a layman to prove special circumstances at his own trial.

It was also unfair, Fortas said, to require a defendant to wait for a ruling by an appeals court to win a fair trial. The defendant would doubtless spend the intervening time in prison. In the meantime, records might be lost; witnesses could disappear.

In the fourth section, the brief established the right to counsel at a criminal trial as the minimum right the Court should establish. Fortas stated his belief that help should be available at all points in criminal proceedings after the arrest. He sidestepped the broader issues of appointment of counsel for arraignment. Arraignment is the stage at which a suspect hears what charges are being filed against him or her and may enter a plea.

Fortas also avoided the question of whether misdemeanors should be included in the Court's directive. He did note that the Court had already ruled that the right to counsel for federal defendants did not extend to petty offenses. Presumably, the states should be held to the same standard.

The final section dealt with the widely held fear that reversing *Betts* would result in the release of many prisoners. Such fears hadn't kept the

Court from making the *Mapp* and *Griffin* decisions. Although these decisions had led to the freeing of some prisoners, there was no ensuing crime wave. Fortas pointed out that anyone convicted without benefit of counsel could always be tried again.

In his summary, Fortas criticized the *Betts* decision as unjust. The rights of Americans were a precious resource to be guarded in a world filled with tyrannical dictatorships, he said. His arguments completed, he formally asked the Court to overturn *Betts* and reverse the Florida court ruling denying Gideon his request for an attorney. An appendix to the brief followed, analyzing Gideon's trial transcript for weaknesses in the defense that could have been corrected by a lawyer.

Fortas turned in his brief to the Court. As required, he sent a copy to Florida's lawyer, Bruce Jacob. Jacob would have the chance to study Fortas's brief for weaknesses before submitting his own. Now the ball was in his court.

Assistant Attorney General Bruce R. Jacob, pictured on a TV screen during an interview

CHAPTER FIVE

Florida Fights Back

*I thought everyone should have a law-
yer, we all thought that. But I thought
the states should do it by themselves,
not have it imposed on them by constitutional construction.[1]*

—Bruce R. Jacob

Assistant Attorney General Bruce R. Jacob recog-
nized the irony in the fact that he was the one selected to represent the
Florida Division of Corrections in Gideon's suit against the state. He had
been chairman of the legal aid society at his law school. Now he would have
to convince the Supreme Court to deny legal aid to a poor man.

Nevertheless, he was honored to be selected by Florida Attorney
General Richard W. Ervin to represent the state in the *Gideon* case. It was
a rare opportunity for someone only three years out of law school to argue
a case before the Supreme Court. Regardless of his personal feelings, Jacob
would try his hardest as advocate for the state.

Jacob first heard of the case when Chief Justice Warren's assistant clerk Michael Rodak Jr. contacted the Florida authorities shortly after Gideon petitioned the Court. The attorney general's office was asked to respond to Gideon's petition. Although not required, such responses help clarify the legal issues and provide additional facts in the case.

Jacob argued that the Court should not hear Gideon's case. He relied entirely on the precedent of *Betts*. Jacob pointed out that there were no special circumstances in Gideon's case. All right-to-counsel cases accepted by the Court since *Betts* had relied on this argument. Gideon hadn't even claimed any particular instances of unfairness at his trial.

Soon after Jacob filed his response, the Court informed him that his recommendation had been denied. The young lawyer began the daunting task of preparing for a Supreme Court hearing. It would not be easy. His counterpart on Gideon's side was a formidable foe.

Fortas had the help of a large, well-established law firm at his disposal. Jacob, inexperienced and overworked, had only himself and what meager resources the underfunded state office could provide. What's more, he had to sandwich his research on *Gideon* that summer around his service in the National Guard, the establishment of a private practice, and his courtship and marriage.

Jacob had two things in his favor. One was the Court's reluctance to overturn previous rulings. The other was the principle of states' rights. Jacob suspected that other states would be sympathetic toward Florida's position. Even if providing attorneys for the poor was state policy, state officials would likely resent federal laws forcing that practice on them. Jacob decided to enlist the help of the other states.

There is a well-established official procedure for soliciting such aid. Interested parties may submit amicus curiae (friend of the court) briefs in any case before the Court. Often, civil liberties watchdogs or other groups promoting social change assist one side or the other. Other persons or groups, though not directly involved in a particular case, realize that a ruling may affect them in the future. An amicus brief is their chance to put in their two cents worth. Such large organizations often have the resources to devote to a case that the litigants, the parties directly involved, cannot afford.

The Court does not have to accept the briefs of private organizations unless the litigants agree to it. Often, such briefs offer little constructive help and serve only as an indication of public opinion. The federal government, through the executive branch's Justice Department, may enter any case. Many times, the Court will seek an opinion from the Justice Department's solicitor general. The federal government has a stake in most cases before the Court. The solicitor general's office has the experience, resources, and expertise to contribute helpful information. States may also file briefs in any case before the Court. They often file briefs in cases involving states' rights.

Jacob sent a letter to the attorneys general in all the other states. He notified them as a request for help in the case and also as a courtesy. Any decision the Court made would affect the other states. Jacob described Gideon's case and the stakes involved. He warned that, should *Betts* be reversed, even misdemeanor cases might require appointed counsel. He hoped that, by raising such fears, he might convince states that currently provided help to felony defendants to go along with him.

Jacob was discouraged with the replies. Half the attorneys general didn't bother to answer. The few who were sympathetic weren't much help. Some were worried about the possibility that the Court might require them to provide counsel to those accused in misdemeanor cases, but they didn't have the money to help in the case. Others were annoyed at further intrusion by the federal government into states' business. The officials in most of those states, however, believed it would be inappropriate to support Florida, since their states already required appointed counsel.

What surprised Jacob was the number of states that wrote back supporting Gideon. Minnesota's attorney general, Walter F. Mondale, was quite blunt in his reply. "I believe in federalism and states' rights, too," he wrote. "But I also believe in the Bill of Rights. . . . Since I firmly believe that any person charged with a felony should be accorded a right to be represented by counsel regardless of his financial condition, I would welcome the courts' imposition of a requirement of appointment of counsel in all state felony prosecutions."[2]

In the end, only Alabama and North Carolina filed an amicus brief supporting Florida's position. It was written by George D. Mentz, assistant attorney general of Alabama. He strongly supported the federalist view that the states had the right to run their own criminal justice systems.

Mentz recognized that American society was moving toward an ideal in which the poor would have the same benefits as wealthier citizens. But he believed that this should be accomplished through social evolution and not government policy. Right to counsel, he argued, would become universal only when the states could afford it. "To be lasting," the brief read, "his [man's] progress must result from his own volition rather than come from judicial fiat."[3]

Mentz also argued that the sympathy of a jury toward an unrepresented defendant was apt to result in a more favorable verdict than if he had a lawyer. Gideon had mounted as competent a defense as the average lawyer, he said. And few lawyers were a match for career prosecutors. Finally, the brief brought up the practical considerations of requiring poor, rural

Justice Arthur J. Goldberg, who replaced Justice Felix Frankfurter on the Court

counties to pay for lawyers in the great number of indigent cases before them.

Gideon's case was delayed several months by Jacob's unsuccessful fight to keep the trial transcript off the record. By the time that issue was settled, Jacob had left the attorney general's office for private practice. Although he had permission to continue working on the case, he had little time. And he had lost an ally on the Court. Justice Felix Frankfurter, one of the staunchest defenders of states' rights, had retired. Arthur J. Goldberg, President John F. Kennedy's appointment to replace Frankfurter, was less likely to support Jacob's position.

Still, Jacob provided a spirited defense of Florida's stand in his brief. Filed in late December, it was divided into two sections. First, Jacob established that Gideon had lawfully been denied counsel under the provisions of *Betts v. Brady*. He established that there had been nothing in Gideon's case that rendered his trial unfair. A review of Supreme Court decisions after *Betts* showed that none of the special circumstances cited applied to Gideon. To support this argument, Jacob included a letter from Judge McCrary stating that he believed Gideon had done "as well as most lawyers could have done in handling his case."[4]

The brief's second section was devoted to arguing against overturning *Betts*. Jacob found no historical basis for requiring that attorneys be provided for poor people. Clearly, the Sixth Amendment had not been written with that in mind. Rather, the founders' intent, Jacob argued, was to revoke the English practice of forbidding counsel to accused felons.

Jacob next made a plea for the freedom of states to run their own criminal justice systems. It was paternalistic of the federal government, he said, to assume that its practices were best. The states should be allowed to experiment with different methods of administering justice. Otherwise, there could be no hope of progress in that field.

The brief argued that the due process clause of the Fourteenth Amendment made no mention of requiring counsel. It required only that the proceedings be fair. The authors had left the wording intentionally vague, he noted, to cover whatever legal practices were accepted for the times. Gideon was not automatically covered by this provision, Jacob argued.

Next, Jacob claimed that *Betts v. Brady* provided a clear framework for judging when counsel needed to be appointed. The special circumstances calling for counsel were plainly listed in subsequent cases. Any inconsistencies in application were due to differing circumstances in the various cases. This was common in the application of any law.

The fact that the majority of the states required provision of counsel to poor people shouldn't sway the judges, Jacob went on. The states had widely different rules for determining when to assign attorneys. Because there was no consensus, Jacob noted, right to counsel could not be considered a fundamental right.

Jacob then moved on to the practical aspects of overturning *Betts*. If the Sixth Amendment applied to the states, poor defendants charged with any crime would be entitled to counsel. Poor people accused of misdemeanors would be more apt to plead not guilty. This would soon tie up the courts. It would be difficult to draw the line at criminal cases, Jacob argued. Poor people being served with civil suits would also demand representation. The expense to the states would be enormous. In some areas, there would not be enough lawyers to handle all the new cases.

If *Betts* was overturned on the basis of equal protection of the law, there would be further problems, according to Jacob. The states would have to provide lawyers for appeals. Public funds would need to be provided for travel expenses, expert witnesses, private investigators. Even bail would have to be set at appropriate levels for the accused's income, Jacob argued.

Finally, Jacob's brief warned of the consequences for past convictions if *Betts* was discarded. About 65 percent of Florida's prisoners had been tried without lawyers. The state's attorney predicted that a crime wave would follow the release of that many convicts.

Jacob was not hopeful of winning. The Court had whittled away at *Betts* almost from the moment it was decided. It was only a matter of time before the Court discarded it entirely. Jacob feared that *Gideon* might be the case that the Court would use to overturn *Betts*. He included one last request in his summary. He asked that, in the event *Betts* was overturned, the Court would apply its decision only to future cases. That way, though Gideon would get a new trial, others already in prison wouldn't be affected by the ruling. Though this was an established legal procedure, it had never been used by the Supreme Court.

Jacob submitted his brief to the Court and hoped for the best.

Three other briefs were filed in the case, all supporting Gideon's side of the arguments. Minnesota Attorney General Walter F. Mondale hadn't forgotten Gideon's appeal after replying to Jacob's request for amicus curiae briefs. He contacted several other state officials for their thoughts on the matter. Massachusetts Attorney General Edward J. McCormack Jr. was one of them. McCormack and his assistant, Gerald A. Berlin, wanted to write an amicus brief supporting Gideon. Mondale approved and enlisted the help of other state attorneys general. Berlin's brief was forwarded to the Court signed by officials of 23 states.

The amicus brief called upon the Court to overturn *Betts*. It was unprecedented for that many states to call upon the Supreme Court to issue an order that would increase federal control over state affairs. The brief was a complete surprise to Fortas, Jacob, and the justices themselves.

In his brief, Berlin was careful to ask the Court to limit the scope of its ruling in the case. He specified that the right to counsel should apply only to felony suspects. State funds, Berlin said, should be used only for legal fees and not for witnesses or expert testimony or traveling expenses. He also suggested that limiting application of the ruling to future cases might be desirable.

The brief ended with an eloquent request:

> *Betts v. Brady*, already an anachronism when
> handed down, has spawned twenty years of bad

Walter F. Mondale, as attorney general of Minnesota, organized support among the states for Gideon's appeal.

law. That in the world of today a man may be condemned to penal servitude for lack of means to supply counsel for his defense is unthinkable. We respectfully urge that the conviction below be reversed, that *Betts v. Brady* be reconsidered, and that this Court require that all persons tried for a felony in a state court shall have the right to counsel as a matter of due process of law and of equal protection of the laws.[5]

Oregon sent in another unexpected brief. In 1959, Oregon had passed a law to allow prisoners to sue in state courts over violations of their federal rights. Fifteen prisoners had won their cases on the basis of their having had no lawyers during their trials. Oregon officials came to realize that it would have been less expensive to provide counsel to begin with than to right the injustice through the appeals process.

The American Civil Liberties Union (ACLU) also participated. J. Lee Rankin, solicitor general under President Dwight D. Eisenhower, had urged the nonprofit civil rights group to file a brief in the case. Rankin was strongly committed to civil liberties and assisted the ACLU with its brief.

The ACLU's main contribution was an analysis of state court decisions on special circumstances appeals. It revealed that of 139 decisions since *Betts*, only 11 found special circumstances requiring appointment of counsel. The brief also noted that habeas corpus petitions such as Gideon's had increased from 127 in the year before *Betts* to 871 in 1960. The number of these petitions asking for federal review of state court decisions was clearly more dangerous to states' rights than would be a mandate for state-appointed counsel.

Everyone's cards were now on the table. Soon the showdown would begin. The participants were told to meet at the Supreme Court on January 14, 1963, for the oral arguments. This was Gideon's last chance to make his case.

CHAPTER SIX

The **Hearing**

I think time has now made it possible for the correct rule, the civilized rule, the rule of American constitutionalism, the rule of due process to be stated by this Court with limited disturbance to the states.[1]

—**Abe Fortas**

Bruce Jacob must have felt very small as he entered the Supreme Court building for the first time on the morning of January 14, 1963. The facade of the Washington, D.C., edifice is gargantuan in scale. Everything is designed to impress the observer with the gravity of the business conducted there. Massive columns reach to the top of marbled halls. Huge bronze gates separate the public areas from the justices' work space. In the courtroom itself, friezes of the great figures of history look down upon the proceedings.

The hearing begins on an equally impressive tone. Everyone stands as the black-robed justices enter the room from behind red velvet curtains.

A photograph shows the courtroom where Supreme Court cases are argued. The justices sit in the leather chairs in back of the wooden bench.

Their bench looks down on the tables for the attorneys and the spectators' seats. The Court crier calls, "Oyez, oyez, oyez," an ancient term warning those present to hear his words. "All persons having business before the honorable, the Supreme Court of the United States, are admonished to draw near and give their attention, for the Court is now sitting. . . ."[2]

Once the hearing is under way, the formality ends. As the advocates argue their case, the atmosphere takes on the quality of a discussion at a local tavern. The justices frequently interrupt, badgering the attorneys with questions. Long-winded speeches are cut short—the advocates are encouraged to present facts, not rhetoric.

The justices impose no such restrictions on themselves. They often ask questions designed to emphasize an issue, rather than to elicit a response. The justices talk among themselves or with their clerks. Sometimes a justice will answer mail, with only half an ear tuned to the lawyers' arguments.[3] The effect is disconcerting for a lawyer appearing before the Court for the first time.

Attorneys have strict time limits in which to present their cases. Those ignoring the flashing red light indicating that their time is over may look up to find an empty bench. Generally, each side is given an hour or a half hour, depending on the complexity of the issues involved, to present its case. The Court granted Fortas and Jacob an hour each. In an unusual move, the Court also granted an extra half hour each for the presentation of Alabama's and the ACLU's amicus briefs.

There is no particular time when arguments begin. Suits are heard in order. When one case is over, the next begins. Litigants are called well in advance, so that the justices won't have to wait.

Other cases took up the Court's time, so arguments in *Gideon v. Cochran* didn't begin until the next morning, January 15. Abe Fortas, because he represented the plaintiff, went first. Fortas began by stating that the right to counsel at a criminal trial for a poor felony defendant was the only issue being debated. He set forth the facts of the case. Fortas described Gideon's alleged crime and his trial.

Fortas conceded that there were no special circumstances that required counsel to be appointed for Gideon. "To me," he told the Court, "this case shows the basic difficulty with *Betts v. Brady*—that no man, however intelligent, can conduct his own defense adequately."[4] Justice John Marshall Harlan interrupted. He didn't believe that was the issue at stake in *Betts*.

Fortas had expected criticism from Harlan. The justice was the strongest advocate of states' rights on the Court. Fortas answered, "I entirely agree, Mr. Justice Harlan, with the point you are making: Namely, that of course a man cannot have a fair trial without a lawyer, but *Betts* held that this consideration was outweighed by the demands of federalism. . . ."[5] Then Fortas moved to the core of his argument. He suggested that states' rights were threatened by the degree of federal scrutiny of state court decisions due to right-to-counsel appeals.

Fortas launched into a history of right-to-counsel cases. He covered the Court's record of finding special circumstances. Then he questioned the courts' ability to determine what constituted a special circumstance. "How can a judge, when a man is arraigned, look at him and say there are special circumstances? Does the judge say, 'You look stupid,' or 'Your case involves complicated facts'? It is administratively unworkable."[6]

Justices Arthur J. Goldberg and Potter Stewart asked how far Fortas thought the Court should go. Should the Court provide counsel for traffic offenses? And at what stage of the criminal proceedings should a lawyer be provided?

J. Lee Rankin, who argued the case for the American Civil Liberties Union

Fortas replied that it wasn't necessary to decide that for this appeal. He pointed out that defendants in federal trials were covered for all but petty crimes. In his opinion, he told the Court, lawyers should be furnished from arraignment through final appeal. He saw no problem in extending to minor crimes the right to counsel. A public defender's office, Fortas said, should be equipped to handle all offenses. Fortas didn't believe many defendants would bother with a lawyer for small matters.

The Court broke for lunch, then returned to question Fortas. Stewart wanted to know if Fortas was arguing that the Fourteenth Amendment was meant to include the protection of the Bill of Rights. Fortas said he was not making that argument. Justice Black, whose beliefs were well known, wanted to know why not. "Mr. Justice Black," Fortas answered, "I like that argument that you have made so eloquently. But I cannot as an advocate make that argument because this Court has rejected it so many times. I hope you never cease making it."[7] The justices and the audience laughed.

J. Lee Rankin appeared next to present the ACLU's side. Amicus arguments tend to emphasize broad principles of law. The principal litigants usually do better discussing the particulars of the case. Rankin concentrated on the unlikelihood of a fair trial for a man representing himself. "It is enough of a fiction to claim that an ordinary lawyer can present a case as well as the prosecutor with all his experience in court. But when you take a layman and put him at odds, you can't have a fair trial except by accident."[8]

Rankin claimed that *Betts* presumed that defendants needed an attorney only in a special case. In fact, he said, it was a special case when they didn't need one. Justice Stewart helped by pointing out that the legal profession assumed a layman wasn't knowledgeable in the law. After all, Stewart said, Gideon wouldn't be allowed to represent anyone else in court.

Rankin finished by asking the Court to apply any ruling overturning *Betts* to both past and future cases. He pooh-poohed the idea that the jails would be emptied of illegally convicted prisoners. Prodded by Harlan, Rankin said he didn't believe a ruling restricted to just future cases would stand up to constitutional scrutiny.

Jacob's turn came next. The inexperienced young lawyer had barely begun when the justices fired questions at him. They never let up during his entire presentation. Justice Black was his chief adversary. He questioned *Betts*'s vagueness on what comprised special circumstances. Jacob replied that each new right-to-counsel case before the Court clarified the issue. Many laws are developed over the years in this way. The Court always issues decisions on as narrow grounds as possible, covering only the precise point of law questioned in a particular appeal.

Justice Brennan reminded Jacob that every Florida right-to-counsel case the Court had decided in recent years had been overturned. Jacob believed that such case-by-case adjudication was preferable to a blanket rule. The states needed wide latitude, he said, in running their criminal justice systems.

Justices Harlan and Stewart drew Jacob into a discussion on why capital cases were singled out as requiring counsel. Jacob admitted there was nothing in the Constitution that made that distinction.

Jacob briefly mentioned the states' historical right to experiment with the way they dealt with crime. Then he moved on to the practical consequences of overruling *Betts*. Such an act would inevitably lead to demands for state-supplied lawyers for even trivial crimes, he argued. Next the poor would expect funding for expert witnesses and private detectives. The cost to taxpayers, he said, would be phenomenal. "In effect, this court would be requiring the states to adopt socialism or a welfare program,"[9] he warned the Court.

Jacob concluded by mentioning the thousands of current Florida prisoners who had been tried without counsel. He asked the Court to limit the ruling in order to keep those men behind bars if *Betts* was overturned. Chief Justice Warren asked how many of those prisoners were illiterate. Jacob didn't know, but agreed that some of them probably were. Warren's point went unsaid, but it was obvious: illiteracy was a special circumstance under the *Betts* rule. Perhaps a favorable ruling for Gideon might provide a chance to correct the injustice that had put those people in jail.

Last up was George Mentz, who discussed the points raised in the amicus brief prepared for Alabama and signed by North Carolina. His main argument was for states' rights. He admitted it wasn't right for anyone to stand trial without a lawyer. But it was the states' province to change the law themselves, he said. Harlan wanted to know how many years that would take. Mentz couldn't say, but he maintained that the states were heading that way.

Mentz claimed that trial judges protected the rights of unrepresented defendants. Stewart told him that wasn't the judge's job. Justice Goldberg pointed out that a judge couldn't provide the final argument to the jury, pleading the defendant's case.

Mentz's last point was that unrepresented defendants probably were better off because the judge and the jury tended to be sympathetic toward them. "The average Alabama lawyer is not equipped to deal with the career prosecutor. An articulate defendant may get his story across to the jury better," he said.

"That's not very complimentary to our profession," Black shot back.

"No sir,"[10] Mentz said with a smile. Justice Douglas suggested sarcastically that if laymen had the advantage, perhaps the Sixth Amendment should be repealed.

Fortas was allowed five minutes to rebut Jacob's and Mentz's arguments. He brought up *Mapp v. Ohio*, hoping to provide a precedent for requiring the states to abide by one of the Bill of Rights amendments. He pleaded with the Court to allow a minimal interference with states' rights in order to serve the cause of justice.

Justice Harlan still had his doubts. He asked Fortas if he had found any flaw in the reasoning of Justice Roberts, the author of *Betts*. Was Roberts's analysis of the historical intent of the nation's founders correct? If not, the Court might have grounds to overturn *Betts*. Fortas admitted that he had found no error in Roberts's appraisal. If the justices were going to overrule *Betts*, they would have to justify their decision some other way.

CHAPTER SEVEN

The Supreme Court

We are under a Constitution, but the Constitution is what the judges say it is.[1]

—Chief Justice Charles Evans Hughes

In setting up a system of law, the founders decided that there must be a final arbiter for all disputes. Otherwise, some questions would never be resolved. Legal issues are always subject to interpretation. If society is to remain stable, the citizens must know that the laws governing them will remain fairly constant from year to year.

Trusting such arbitration to the executive or legislative branch wouldn't be effective. The U.S. administration can change its head every four years, as new presidents are elected. The legislature is constantly changing its direction. Members of the House of Representatives face reelection every other year. Senate terms are for six years.

It is the executive branch that most directly controls the lives of U.S. citizens by enforcing the laws. There is a danger in allowing the nation's leaders the power to interpret those laws as well. The many dictatorships in the world's history teach that lesson.

The legislature can change or revoke a law if it disagrees with its interpretation. That power is spread too thinly, though, to carry much danger of despotism. To gain approval from hundreds of members of Congress facing reelection, laws must meet public approval. Some issues are so divisive they will never be resolved by such a large body.

It is these issues that dictate the structure of the Supreme Court. Members of the Court are appointed by the president, but must be confirmed by the Senate. Justices' terms are for life, to make them almost immune to political considerations.

Justices may be impeached (brought to trial) by a majority vote of the House of Representatives. Trial is held before the Senate. If found guilty of serious offenses by a two-thirds vote of the Senate, a justice may be removed from office. Impeachment proceedings of a Supreme Court justice has happened only once, when Justice Samuel Chase was unsuccessfully impeached in 1805. The process of impeachment and conviction is extremely difficult. It requires the consensus of so many people that only justices guilty of major crimes can be successfully removed from office.

The number of Supreme Court justices varied throughout its early years. Today, the Court's power is concentrated in the hands of nine justices. This number is large enough to provide a diversity of experience and views, but small enough to work well.

Cases reach the Supreme Court in three ways. Some cases, such as disputes between states, or between a state and a foreign nation, are mandated by the Constitution to go before the Court. State laws challenged as unconstitutional may be sent up from a circuit court of appeals. Most cases, like Gideon's, arrive by a writ of certiorari. At least four of the justices must vote that a case deserves a hearing. Almost all requests for "cert" are denied. Sometimes the justices believe there are no substantial issues of federal or constitutional law involved. In other cases, they believe

Earl Warren, pictured here speaking on board the *Polaris* missile-firing submarine, was chief justice of the Supreme Court when Gideon brought his case to the Court.

the question has already been settled by a prior Supreme Court decision. The Court will refuse to hear cases that are political in nature or that threaten the separation of the powers dictated by the Constitution.

The Court will not give an advisory opinion. It issues rulings only on cases presented before the Court. George Washington was the first president to ask for an advisory opinion. The Court turned him down. Only parties with standing—a practical stake in the matter—can bring a suit to the Court.

The Court tries to follow a policy of judicial self-restraint. Opinions issued by the Court will address only the matter at hand. The justices avoid deciding broad issues of law. This gives the Court greater flexibility in dealing with related questions at a later date. Slightly different circumstances may call for different solutions, but the Court tries to avoid overturning one of its own decisions.

The Court reaches its decisions by a simple majority. Sometimes justices must remove themselves from a case if there is a conflict of interest in a particular case. At times the death or resignation of a justice will leave a temporary vacancy. If this results in an even number on the Court, and a tie vote is reached in a case, the tie results in upholding whatever decision is being appealed.

The chief justice assigns a single member of the Court to write the opinion reflecting the views of the majority. If the chief justice was in the minority, then the right to assign the opinion falls to the justice on the majority side who has served the longest.

Any individual justice is allowed to attach a dissent, disagreeing with the majority opinion. A justice may add a concurrence, agreeing with the decision, but differing in its scope or the reasoning behind it. A justice may also co-sign another's dissent or concurrence. Dissenting and concurring opinions have no legal effect on the issue at hand; the majority opinion carries the full weight of the law. They may be cited at a later date, though, to support the arguments of another case. Chief Justice Hughes once said, "A dissent in a court of last resort is an appeal to the brooding spirit of the law, to the intelligence of a future day, when a later decision may possibly correct the error into which the dissenting judge believes the court to have been betrayed."[2]

The Court usually holds sessions from October to late June or early July. Hearings are held Monday through Thursday. Fridays are reserved for the justices' conference, when they discuss the cases heard during the week. Often they take an initial vote then. Final decisions are announced on Mondays.

The Friday conferences are held in secrecy. The justices sit at a long oak table surrounded by bookshelves filled with thousands of law volumes. Not even their clerks attend the conferences. It is the duty of the most junior member of the Court, the justice who has served the shortest amount of time, to run errands. The justices speak in order of seniority, with the chief justice going first. Each in turn offers his or her opinion of the cases on the agenda. Then, in reverse order, they vote. This is to keep junior members from being swayed by the opinions of their more respected seniors.

Usually the justices will have reached their decisions before they hear the oral arguments. The written briefs contain the facts of the case and the relevant precedents. The justices allow themselves ample time to study the issues before the hearing. Nevertheless, they allow the advocates the chance to persuade them during the orals. Occasionally, in the give-and-take of argument, questioning, and rebuttal, new perspectives are gained. Because the hearings are covered by the press, the Court is well aware of public reaction to the case under scrutiny.

The process of arriving at a consensus, voting, and writing the opinions often takes months. Drafts are written and rewritten; votes are changed as the justices research the issues. There is no prior announcement of which decisions will be read on any given Monday. The justices who write the majority opinions read their own decisions. Most courts issue only written opinions. Perhaps because its decisions are final, the Supreme Court has kept the tradition of oral announcements. The importance of its business and the accountability of the justices to the people are thus emphasized.

Clarence Gideon in 1979

On March 18, 1963, after deliberating Gideon's case for two months, the Supreme Court entered the chamber to announce its verdict. In a unanimous vote, the Court ruled that *Betts* should be overturned. Gideon had won!

Justice Black, the chief dissenter in *Betts* 21 years earlier, had been assigned the opinion. Black's opinion spoke of the continuing controversy since *Betts* had been decided. He noted the similarity between Betts's and Gideon's cases. Plainly, for Gideon to win his appeal, the Court had to reverse its prior decision.

Black's ruling accepted the principle, stated in *Betts*, that the Fourteenth Amendment forced the states to grant citizens those rights considered "fundamental and essential to a fair trial."[3] Black noted that the Court had declared the right to counsel to be one of those rights in *Powell v. Alabama*, ten years before *Betts*. Because the decision in *Powell* was limited to that particular case, subsequent Courts weren't obliged to abide by that verdict. Despite that fact, *Powell's* "conclusions about the fundamental nature of the right to counsel are unmistakable,"[4] Black noted.

The opinion mentioned *Johnson v. Zerbst*, and other precedents supporting the right to counsel. Black wrote:

> The Court in *Betts v. Brady* made an abrupt
> break with its own well-considered precedents.
> In returning to these old precedents . . . we but
> restore constitutional principles established to
> achieve a fair system of justice. Not only these
> precedents but also reason and reflection
> require us to recognize that in our adversary
> system of criminal justice, any person haled
> into court, who is too poor to hire a lawyer,
> cannot be assured a fair trial unless counsel is
> provided for him. This seems to us to be an
> obvious truth.[5]

There were three concurrences. Justice Tom Clark supported the opinion of the Court because it did not distinguish between capital and noncapital cases for the purposes of appointing counsel. If the Fourteenth Amendment guaranteed counsel when one's life was at stake, as *Powell* had determined, then it must do the same when one's liberty or property were threatened, Clark said.

Justice Douglas thought that the Court's opinion didn't go far enough. His concurrence argued that the privileges of the entire Bill of Rights were protected by the Fourteenth Amendment. Recognizing that he was in the minority, Douglas nevertheless noted, "All constitutional questions are always open. And what we do today does not foreclose the matter."[6]

Justice Harlan, though concurring, disagreed with the Court's conclusion that *Betts* was an improper decision. He noted that the decision had established that the right to counsel should be assured under special circumstances. While agreeing that *Johnson v. Zerbst* had given the right of counsel to federal defendants, "to have imposed these requirements on the States would indeed have been 'an abrupt break' with the almost immediate past."[7]

But Harlan recognized that special circumstances had come to include so wide a variety of conditions that the *Betts* ruling was becoming meaningless. "To continue a rule which is honored by this Court only with lip service is not a healthy thing and in the long run will do disservice to the federal system,"[8] he concluded.

Gideon's case was ordered back to the Supreme Court of Florida. Florida officials had no choice but to set a new trial for Gideon. Gideon's battle continued, but his mark had already been made on history.

CHAPTER EIGHT

Gideon's Second Trial

It has become almost axiomatic that the great rights which are secured for all of us by the Bill of Rights are constantly tested and retested in the courts by the people who live in the bottom of society's barrel. . . . Upon the shoulders of such persons are our great rights carried.[1]

—Tobias Simon

When news of Gideon's victory reached the prison at Raiford, he became a hero among the prisoners. "The majority of the men in there with me had been convicted without a lawyer to defend them," said Gideon, "and nine out of ten saw a way of getting out if I did."[2]

Gideon was grateful to Abe Fortas for winning his appeal. He agreed when Fortas suggested that a Florida ACLU lawyer, Tobias Simon, represent him at his retrial. Gideon wrote to Simon, asking for his help.

After almost two years in jail for the poolroom robbery, Gideon was bitter. He had thought that the Florida Supreme Court would set him free immediately. Instead, the court returned the case to the Bay County

Clarence Gideon playing pool in 1979

Circuit Court for rescheduling. Gideon thought the court was abusing his civil rights again. Trying a person twice for the same crime is known as double jeopardy, which is forbidden by the Fifth Amendment. This does not apply to cases that have been successfully appealed, however. The distinction was not clear to Gideon.

When Simon arrived at Gideon's prison to interview him before the trial, the attorney found him uncooperative. Gideon had discovered that he would be tried before the same judge in the same courtroom. He was convinced that he could not get a fair trial. By July 4, 1963, the day before the trial, Gideon had refused to let Simon or anyone else represent him.

In court the next morning, Gideon told Judge McCrary that he wanted to file to move the trial to another court. He wanted to act as his own attorney and plainly mistrusted anyone connected with the judicial system.

The irony of Gideon's fighting a two-year battle to have counsel and then refusing it was not lost on Judge McCrary. Nevertheless, he was determined to protect Gideon's best interests. McCrary dismissed Simon and told Gideon he could not represent himself. Gideon still had no money to hire his own counsel. McCrary asked Gideon if there were any lawyers to his liking. Gideon named W. Fred Turner, a local attorney. The judge agreed that Florida would pay Turner to represent Gideon.

Florida had already complied with the Supreme Court ruling by assigning a public defender to the circuit court. One of the prosecutor's assistants suggested that the new appointee help out Turner. Gideon wouldn't hear of it.

Judge McCrary advised Gideon to contact his new lawyer in order to file his motion to move the trial. Gideon replied, "If I'm going back to the penitentiary for the same crime, I want to do it my way. I want to file my own motions."[3]

Gideon proceeded to read to the court two motions he had written. He said that he should be freed due to the double jeopardy protection of the Fifth Amendment. He also claimed to be protected from a new trial by Florida's two-year statute of limitations on minor crimes. More than two years had passed since the burglary, but the law didn't apply to retrials won by appeal.

McCrary told Gideon he would rule on the motions later. Then he set the new trial date for August 5. The judge ruled against Gideon's motions on August 1. He also turned down motions introduced by Turner to dismiss the charges.

Fred Turner had readily agreed to represent Gideon, despite the defendant's erratic and uncooperative attitude. Turner spent three days before the trial researching the facts of the case. He interviewed the witnesses and even helped Henry Cook's mother pick pears while quizzing her about her son. He already knew most of the locals in the small town of Bay Harbor. Turner had served as Cook's lawyer in the past, defending him on a robbery charge and in a divorce action.

The first business the morning of the trial was to choose the jury. Assistant State Attorney William E. Harris was again Gideon's prosecutor. Now that Gideon's case was high-profile, Harris was joined by his boss, J. Frank Adams. Adams was cynical about Gideon's chances. "If he'd had a lawyer in the first place, he'd have been advised to plead guilty,"[4] Adams said.

Harris accepted the first six men called from the jury pool. Turner, however, rejected two of them. He was familiar with them and knew one was a teetotaler and the other was a convicter, someone who would most likely vote to convict the defendant.

Henry Cook was called to the stand first. He repeated what he had said at the first trial. He told the court he had been at a dance in another city. His friends had left him outside the poolroom where he saw Gideon, he said.

Turner began his questioning. He wanted to know why Cook was dropped off two blocks from his house. Cook answered uneasily that he had planned to wait there for the poolroom to open—an hour and a half later. Turner saw his opening. He asked Cook if he had gone into the poolroom to get beer. Cook denied it. Turner wanted to know how Cook could have seen Gideon inside the building when the windows were blocked by posters. Cook had no answer.

The attorney asked if Cook had ever been convicted of a felony—the same question Gideon had asked him. Cook said no, but he admitted he had received probation for a car theft. Turner and Harris sparred for a bit over whether Cook had lied when he denied being a felon at the first trial. This was important in establishing Cook's reliability as a witness. Cook said he hadn't understood the question.

Next up was Ira Strickland, the poolroom operator. This time around, Turner elicited the admission that Strickland sometimes had allowed Gideon to run the poolroom for him.

After lunch, the detective who had arrested Gideon was called to the stand. Duell Pitts reported that 28 bottles of beer, wine, and soda and about $65 from the vending machines were missing from the poolroom after the break-in. Turner wanted to know what Pitts had found on Gideon when he arrested him a few hours later. Gideon was carrying slightly over $25 in change.

Preston Bray, the cabdriver who gave Gideon a ride that morning, told Harris that Gideon had asked him not to tell anyone that he had seen him. That seemed suspicious, but upon cross-examination by Turner, he said that Gideon often made that request. Bray believed that was due to

Gideon's troubles with his wife. He also remembered that Gideon carried no bottles, and his pockets didn't bulge.

The prosecution concluded its case. Turner asked for a dismissal. The state had presented no evidence that Gideon had broken into the poolroom, only that he had been in there. And there were no stolen goods recovered. Judge McCrary turned down Turner's request to dismiss the case.

Now it was the defense's turn. Turner called J. D. Henderson to the stand. Henderson hadn't testified at the first trial and was there because of Turner's detective work. Henderson told the court that Cook had come into his Bay Harbor grocery store the morning of the burglary. Cook had told Henderson that the police had picked him up for questioning about the break-in. Then Cook told the grocer that he had seen someone inside, but he wasn't sure who it was. Henderson testified that Cook had said only that it "looked like Mr. Gideon."[5] This wasn't the positive identification reported in the first trial.

Turner's only other witness was Gideon himself. Turner began by asking Gideon if he had broken into and robbed the poolroom. Gideon denied it. He said he'd gone into town to buy something to drink. Turner asked where Gideon had gotten the money. Gideon said it was from gambling.

As for the missing merchandise, Gideon claimed to know nothing about it. He said he didn't even drink wine. All he'd done, he said, was buy beer and vodka in town that morning.

Turner turned his witness over to the state. Harris established that Gideon was unemployed at the time of the burglary. He painted rooms at the Bay Harbor Hotel in exchange for free rent. He also made a little money running poker games in the poolroom for Strickland.

The prosecutor then wanted to know why Gideon's money was all in coins. "I've had as much as one hundred dollars in my pockets in coins," Gideon answered.

"Why?" Harris wanted to know.

Gideon appeared puzzled. "Have you ever run a poker game?" he asked the prosecutor.

"You would carry one hundred dollars in coins around for a couple of days at a time?" Harris asked.

"Yes, sir," Gideon answered, "I sure wouldn't leave it in a room in the Bay Harbor Hotel."[6]

The lawyers now were ready to make their closing statements. The defense attorney went first. Turner pointed out that Cook's actions were a bit strange. Officer Berryhill had found him waiting outside the poolroom at 5:30 in the morning with no good explanation for his presence. He claimed to have seen Gideon in the building and followed him to a phone booth, and yet he didn't notify the police. And what had happened to all the beer, wine, and soda?

Turner made his final point to the jury. "Why was Cook walking back and forth? I'll give you the explanation: He was the lookout."[7] Turner accused Cook and his friends of robbing the poolroom. Gideon, he claimed, was simply in the wrong place at the wrong time. Cook had seen him, and, when caught outside the poolroom by the police, he blamed the crime on Gideon.

In rebuttal, Harris reminded the jury that no evidence was presented to prove that Cook and his friends were guilty. The prosecutor did his best to cast doubt on Gideon's story that the change in his pockets was from a card game. "Do you believe that?"[8] Harris asked the jury with raised eyebrows.

Evidently, they did. At Turner's request, Judge McCrary instructed the jury that they must find Gideon guilty beyond a reasonable doubt. The jurors left the room to debate Gideon's possible guilt among themselves. In an hour, they returned to the courtroom. The verdict was not guilty.

Clarence Earl Gideon was a free man. His two-year battle had not been in vain. Turner had been thorough in his detective work and skillful in his presentation. It is possible that Gideon's last-minute choice of a local lawyer had made the difference. The jury might have been suspicious of the tactics of a big-city lawyer.

Gideon visited the Bay Harbor Poolroom that night in triumph. The next day he visited his children. His name cleared, a new life awaited him.

CHAPTER NINE

The Right-to-Counsel Today

There can be no equal justice where the kind of trial a man gets depends on the amount of money he has.[1]

—Justice Hugo L. Black

The months after Gideon's appeal saw great upheaval in the states' justice systems. The chairman of the National Legal Aid and Defender Society called the Court's decision the beginning of "a revolution in the administration of criminal justice in this country."[2] Overall, the decision was well received. Still, the states had to scramble to pass laws to bring them into line with the *Gideon* decision.

Legislators introduced bills to create public defender offices or pay for private attorneys. Rosters of bar members were drawn up to provide rotating pools from which judges could appoint lawyers. Anticipating that the right to counsel would be extended beyond felony trials, several states had begun to appoint attorneys for poor people in misdemeanor cases and appeals even before Gideon's retrial.

In the remainder of their 1962 term, the Supreme Court justices reversed 31 other convictions appealed because the defendant had had no counsel. One of those cases was that of an illiterate Florida prisoner who had been helped with his appeal by Clarence Gideon.

The Supreme Court began expanding the situations where people were guaranteed the right to counsel. A case decided the same day as *Gideon* directed that a poor California convict was entitled to a state-supplied lawyer for his appeal. Later in the term, the Court ruled that a Maryland man should have had an attorney at a preliminary hearing after his arrest to help him with his plea.

By the beginning of the Court's next term, more than 3,000 of the 4,500 Florida prisoners who had been tried without counsel had appealed their convictions. Ten of those prisoners' appeals found their way to the Supreme Court. On October 14, 1963, the Court directed Florida to reconsider their cases with the *Gideon* ruling in mind.

Many of the Florida cases could not be retried. Officials had lost track of witnesses and disposed of evidence. Record keeping had been shoddy. By May of the following year, more than 1,000 convicts were released outright. Hundreds more won the right to new trials. Eventually, almost 2,000 prisoners won their freedom.

Meanwhile, the federal government tried to improve the mechanisms for providing counsel to the poor. Before *Gideon*, federal judges used no consistent measures to appoint counsel. There was no funding for public defenders or investigative services. Appointed counsel served without pay. They were not reimbursed for their expenses. Frequently, they were appointed long after the arrest, when it was difficult to find witnesses. Few lawyers tried hard to defend their clients under these conditions. Usually, such undesirable jobs went to the newest and most inexperienced lawyers.

Attorney General Robert F. Kennedy in Washington, D.C., in March 1964

As a result of these conditions, the legal aid available to poor people was often mediocre.

Attorney General Robert F. Kennedy appointed a commission to study the problem. It proposed legislation that passed as the Criminal Justice Act of 1964 after the *Gideon* decision. Federal district courts were to choose from two methods to defend the poor. They could pay private attorneys to represent poor people. Or they could compensate legal aid societies for the work they had formerly volunteered. Financial help was provided as the defendant and case required; funds were available for detective work, expert witnesses' fees, and other expenses. Counsel was provided from the time of the preliminary hearing through appeal.

The rights of the accused have been expanded and refined in the years since *Gideon. Escobedo v. Illinois*, decided in 1964, ruled that a suspect is entitled to a lawyer as soon as "the investigation is no longer a general inquiry into an unsolved crime but has begun to focus on a particular suspect."[3] The 1966 case *Miranda v. Arizona* established that police must inform suspects of their rights immediately after arrest, including their right to an appointed attorney if they can't afford to hire one.

The right to competent trial was established by a Supreme Court decision in 1984. Sandra Day O'Connor, the Court's first female justice, wrote the opinion. For a retrial to be granted, two conditions must hold. The attorney's performance must be below prevailing professional norms. And the defendant must prove that, had the lawyer been competent, the outcome of the trial would have been different.

The Criminal Justice Act did much to correct injustices in the federal justice system. Correcting problems on the state level is more difficult. States try many more criminal cases than do federal courts. State defendants tend to be poorer. About one-third of federal defendants need appointed counsel. Twice as many in state cases are poor. Many people who hire lawyers plea-bargain cases or have charges dismissed before trial. At the trial level in state courts, almost 90 percent of the defendants are poor.

Money for public defense comes from state, county, or city sources. Each jurisdiction sets the level of funding and allocates the money. State or local courts typically use one or a combination of three methods to provide

Five young defendants stand in court behind their attorneys. Under the *Gideon* ruling, all defendants are entitled to a lawyer, regardless of their ability to pay for one.

counsel to poor people. The courts can pay private attorneys a set fee or an hourly rate for each case. They can contract with a law firm to handle all cases for those who cannot pay an attorney. Or they can hire a permanent staff of public defenders.

There are pros and cons to any of these methods. Contract lawyers are usually selected by the lowest bid. This is good for the finances of cash-strapped local governments. However, low pay often means that the attorney won't spend as much time or effort on the case. Some lawyers use contract funds to cover office expenses while concentrating on more profitable private practices.

Public defenders have access to resources usually available only to the prosecutor's office. In many places, they are paid almost as much as the state's attorneys. Certainly, they can gain the expertise in criminal law that comes with long experience. However, public defenders cannot handle all the court cases involving poor people. Sometimes two defendants in a case will testify against each other. There would be a conflict of interest in defending both suspects. In that case, a private lawyer must be appointed for at least one of the defendants.

Private attorneys tend to work harder to win their cases. Government control of the public defender's office discourages novel defense tactics. Usually, attorneys for the poor are drawn from a rotating list of all available members of the bar. This method gives private lawyers experience in practicing criminal law. Typical law-school instruction does little to train students for criminal practice.

Criminal law is not as lucrative as corporate law or civil suits. Most lawyers try to avoid the jammed dockets and low pay. Attorneys rarely receive more than $25 an hour for their work, a quarter of their usual fees. In places where lawyers receive a set fee, defending capital crimes may pay from $400 to $1,500 per case. With set fees, lawyers who spend the time needed for such complex cases sometimes receive as little as $3 an hour for their work. As a Detroit lawyer recently put it, "The more time you spend on a case, the less money you make."[4]

Today, almost all state and federal criminal cases are covered by the right to counsel. As long as a charge carries a possible jail sentence, poor people have the right to an attorney in felonies, misdemeanors, and traffic citations. Even in some civil cases, such as mental health commitments and child protection cases, poor people are entitled to counsel. Attorneys are provided throughout the preliminary hearings, indictment, trial, and one appeal.

Often, this is not enough. Even capital cases are covered by public funds only through the first appeals process. Further appeals are sometimes handled by legal aid societies. One such volunteer is Esther Lardent of the American Bar Association's Post Conviction Death Penalty Representation Project. She describes a case where a man 12 hours away from being executed was freed because a volunteer attorney discovered evidence that led the state to drop its case. "Sometimes it is only at this final stage before execution," Lardent says, "that errors at the trial level are uncovered, errors like prosecutorial misconduct and suppression of evidence that might have affected the outcome in the defendant's favor."[5]

Incompetent defenders plague the system. But even if a defendant's attorney is guilty of shoddy defense work, that doesn't mean he or she will win an appeal of the case. Convicts have appealed recent cases because their lawyers fell asleep during testimony or used narcotics or drank heavily throughout trials. Their appeals were denied because they couldn't prove that they would have won their cases otherwise.

Public funding for expert fees, detectives, and the like is meager.

86 Actor Henry Fonda, left, talks with actor-producer John Houseman during a break in filming *Gideon's Trumpet*, based on Clarence Gideon's Supreme Court case that requires states to provide attorneys for poor defendants.

Defenders usually must apply to the judge for these funds. Unless the funds are for a capital case, most judges are reluctant to spend taxpayers' money. The situation is worse in poor rural districts, where defenders must drive miles to work on cases.

The public defense system has its success stories. Although only 15 percent of legal aid cases make it to trial, more than 80 percent of those are won. A recent study by the National Center for State Courts determined that overall, "Indigent defenders get the job done and done well."[6] The center found about the same rate of successful cases among public defenders as among private attorneys.

The situation in the nation's cities is more grim. The recent wars on crime and drugs have jammed the courtrooms with poor defendants. There are 13 million criminal cases in the U.S. every year. Public defenders in major cities spend an average of only 22 hours before trials for major crimes to question witnesses, research legal issues, and prepare paperwork. Suspects in minor offenses may have only 15 minutes of their defender's time. Some public defenders encourage guilty pleas and plea bargaining to save time and effort, regardless of their clients' guilt or innocence. The social consequences go beyond injustice for individuals. Poor people learn disrespect for a justice system that shuffles them aside.

Anthony Lewis, the original reporter for the *New York Times* on the *Gideon* case, recently summed up the nation's right-to-counsel state of affairs.

> In the three decades since Clarence Earl
> Gideon won in the Supreme Court and then,
> with a lawyer, was acquitted by a jury, the
> romance of his case has worn somewhat thin.

We have more public defenders now, and more lawyers appointed to represent poor defendants. But the reality remains that most of those defendants—including those on trial for their lives—get less than the best legal help. Lawyers often have only minutes to prepare their case and little or no money to hire experts or investigators, much less to compensate themselves. The well-to-do who are charged with crime would hardly accept such limits on their right to paid counsel. Notwithstanding the promise of *Gideon v. Wainwright*, our society has a long way to go before it lives up to its motto of equal justice under law.[7]

And what of the heroes of our story? Abe Fortas went on to become a Supreme Court justice. Appointed by President Lyndon Johnson in 1965, he served until his resignation in 1969. Fortas died in 1982.

Gideon remarried and continued to work at a variety of jobs. He died in 1972. A best-selling book and a movie were made about his case. Some of the proceeds went to his children. For the most part, he was unimpressed with his fame. He felt his victory was only what he, or any poor man, deserved. Still, occasionally he felt rewarded for his tenacity in pursuing justice for himself. Shortly after his trial, a young man and his wife stopped Gideon in Panama City, Florida. "You're Gideon, aren't you?" the man asked. "I should thank you. You just got me out of prison." Gideon smiled. "That made me feel pretty good,"[8] he said.

Source Notes

Chapter One

1. Anthony Lewis, *Gideon's Trumpet* (New York: Random House, 1964), p. 78.
2. Ibid., p. 10.
3. Ibid., p. 10.
4. Ibid., p. 57.
5. Michael Durham, "How Gideon Changed High Court's Mind," *Life*, vol. 56 (June 12, 1964), p. 86.
6. Lewis, p. 33.
7. Ibid., p. 98.
8. Arthur S. Link, Robert V. Remini, Douglas Greenberg, and Robert C. McMath Jr., *A Concise History of the American People* (Arlington Heights, Ill.: Harlan Davidson, Inc., 1984), p. A-10.
9. Lewis, pp. 7-8.

Chapter Two

1. Lewis, p. 104.
2. Link, p. A-7.
3. Ibid., p. 89.
4. Link, p. A-10.
5. Ibid., p. A-9.

Chapter Three

1. Lewis, p. 109.
2. Ibid., p. 107.

3. Ibid., p. 108.

4. *New York Times* (June 2, 1942), p. 15.

5. Lewis, p. 112.

6. *New York Times* (Aug. 2, 1942), Section IV, p. 6.

7. Lewis, p. 113.

8. Dorothy Marquardt, *A Guide to the Supreme Court* (New York: Bobbs-Merrill, 1977), p. 15.

Chapter Four

1. Lewis, p. 146.

2. Ibid., pp. 145-146.

3. Ibid., p. 153.

4. Ibid., p. 157.

Chapter Five

1. Lewis, p. 119.

2. Ibid., pp. 37-38.

3. Ibid., p. 126.

4. Ibid., p. 128.

5. Ibid., p. 149.

Chapter Six

1. *New York Times* (Jan. 16, 1963), p. 8.

2. Lewis, p. 167.

3. Bernard Schwartz, *Swann's Way: The School Busing Case and the Supreme Court* (New York: Oxford University Press, 1986), p. 97.

4. *New York Times* (Jan. 16, 1963), p. 8.

5. Lewis, pp. 170-171.

6. Ibid., p. 172.

7. Ibid., p. 174.

8. Ibid., p. 175.

9. Ibid., p. 178.

10. Ibid., pp. 179-180.

Chapter Seven

1. Harold W. Chase and Craig R. Ducat, *Constitutional Interpretation: Cases—Essays—Materials* (St. Paul, Minn.: West, 1974), p. 1.

2. Lewis, p. 183.

3. Maureen Harrison and Steve Gilbert, eds. "Gideon v. Wainwright," in *Landmark Decisions of the United States Supreme Court* (Beverly Hills, Cal., Excellent Books, 1991), p. 56.

4. Ibid., p. 58.

5. Ibid., p. 59.

6. Lewis, p. 190.

7. Chase, p. 966.

8. Lewis, p. 191.

Chapter Eight

1. Lewis, pp. 227-228.

2. Durham, Life, p. 88.

3. Lewis, p. 227.

4. Ibid., p. 229.

5. *New York Times* (Aug. 6, 1963), p. 21.

6. Lewis, p. 236.

7. Ibid., p. 237.

8. Ibid., p. 237.

Chapter Nine

1. Lewis, p. 126.

2. *New York Times* (June 11, 1963), p. 13.

3. Chase, p. 972.

4. Jill Smolowe, "The Trials of the Public Defender," *Time*, vol. 141 (Mar. 29, 1993), p. 50.

5. George M. Anderson, "Defending the Poor: A Harder Task," *America*, vol. 160 (Jan. 14, 1989), p. 6.

6. Ted Gest, "One Poor Man's Legacy," *U.S. News & World Report*, vol. 114 (March 22, 1993), p. 19.

7. Personal letter from Anthony Lewis to author, May 17, 1994.

8. Durham, *Life*, p. 88.

Further Reading

Coy, Harold, (revised by Lorna Greenberg). *The Supreme Court*. New York: Watts, 1981.

David, Andrew. *Famous Supreme Court Cases*. Minneapolis: Lerner, 1980.

Douglas, William O. *The Court Years, 1939-1975: The Autobiography of William O. Douglas*. New York: Random House, 1980.

Force, Eden. *The American Heritage History of the Bill of Rights: The Sixth Amendment*. Englewood Cliffs, New Jersey: Silver Burdett Press, 1991.

Forte, David F. *The Supreme Court*. New York: Watts, 1979.

Fribourg, Marjorie G. *The Supreme Court in American History: Ten Great Decisions—The People, the Times and the Issues*. Philadelphia: Macrae Smith, 1965.

Goldberg, Arthur J. *Equal Justice: The Warren Era of the Supreme Court*. New York: Farrar, Straus & Giroux, 1971.

Goode Stephen. *The Controversial Court: Supreme Court Influences on American Life*. New York: Messner, 1982.

Greene, Carol. *The Supreme Court*. Chicago: Childrens Press, 1985.

Habenstreit, Barbara. *Changing America and the Supreme Court*. New York: Messner, 1970.

Harrison, Maureen, and Steve Gilbert, eds. *Landmark Decisions of the United States Supreme Court*. Beverly Hills, Cal.: Excellent Books, 1991.

Lawson, Don. *Landmark Supreme Court Cases*. Hillside, New Jersey: Enslow, 1987.

Lewis, Anthony. *Gideon's Trumpet*. New York: Random House, 1964.

——. *Clarence Earl Gideon and the Supreme Court*. New York: Random House, 1972.

Marquardt, Dorothy A. *A Guide to the Supreme Court*. Indianapolis: Bobbs-Merrill, 1977.

Norris, Clarence, and Sybil D. Washington. *The Last of the Scottsboro Boys: An Autobiography*. New York: Putnam, 1979.

Patterson, Haywood, and Earl Conrad. *Scottsboro Boy*. Garden City, New York: Doubleday, 1950.

Peterson, Helen Stone. *The Supreme Court in America's Story*. Scarsdale, New York: Garrard, 1976.

Stein, R. Conrad. *The Story of the Powers of the Supreme Court*. Chicago: Childrens Press, 1989.

Tresolini, Rocco. *Historic Decisions of the Supreme Court*. Philadelphia: Lippincott, 1963.

Weaver, John D. *Warren: The Man, the Court, the Era*. Boston: Little, Brown, 1967.

Woodward, Bob, and Scott Armstrong. *The Brethren: Inside the Supreme Court*. New York: Avon Books, 1981.

Index